D0952790

ANIMAL PLANET

HORSES!

BRENDA SCOTT ROYCE

HORSES!

Published by Liberty Street,
an imprint of Time Inc. Books,
a division of Meredith Corporation
225 Liberty Street
New York, NY 10281

LIBERTY
STREET

LIBERTY STREET is a trademark of Time Inc.

ISBN: 978-1-68330-076-2
Library of Congress Control Number: 2017959307

First edition, 2018
1 QGV 18
10 9 8 7 6 5 4 3 2 1

Produced by Scout Books & Media Inc

We welcome your comments and suggestions about Time Inc. Books.
Please write to us at:

Time Inc. Books
Attention: Book Editors
P.O. Box 62310, Tampa, FL 33662-2310
(800) 765-6400

timeincbooks.com

Time Inc. Books products may be purchased for business or
promotional use. For information on bulk purchases, please contact
Christi Crowley in the Special Sales Department at (845) 895-9858.

There is a glossary at the end of this book. This is
an alphabetical list of words and their definitions.
The first time a word that is in the glossary is
used, it appears in **bold**.

CONTENTS

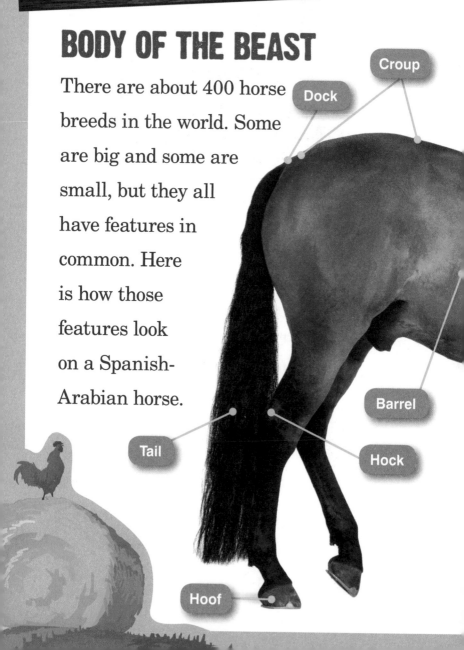

BODY OF THE BEAST

There are about 400 horse breeds in the world. Some are big and some are small, but they all have features in common. Here is how those features look on a Spanish-Arabian horse.

Croup

Dock

Barrel

Tail

Hock

Hoof

Ears

Mane

Withers

Forelock

Shoulder

Muzzle

Knee

A horse's height is measured in "hands," from the ground to the **withers**. A hand equals 4 inches. So a 5-foot-tall (60 inches) horse is said to be 15 hands high.

BEAUTIFUL BEASTS Some horses, such as this mustang, live in the wild. Others are tame animals that live or work with people.

WHAT MAKES A HORSE A HORSE?

The world is full of all kinds of horses. They come in many different sizes. Some are the size of large dogs. Others are as big as bulls. Horses have different strengths, speeds, and styles, too. Workhorses are strong and stout. Racehorses are slim and fast. Show horses are graceful and can look quite fancy. So what makes a horse a horse?

Horses are mammals. Mammals are **vertebrates** (VUR-tuh-britz). This means every mammal has a spinal column, or backbone. Cats, dogs, dolphins, and people are mammals, too. A mammal baby drinks its mother's milk. Also, at some stage in their lives, all mammals have hair or fur on some part of their bodies.

From tiny Shetland ponies to mighty Clydesdales, all horses belong to the same **species**, *Equus ferus*. They all share similar features. A horse has long teeth. A horse's eyes are located high on its long head, with its ears above. The horse can **rotate** its ears without even moving its head. It does this to locate the source of a sound it hears. The long hair on the back of a horse's neck is its mane. The mane is thicker than the rest of the horse's coat.

Mammals with hooves are divided into two types: even-toed and odd-toed. *Odd-toed* doesn't mean their toes look funny. It describes the number of toes on each foot. A horse has just one toe—a hoof—on each foot. That means it is an odd-toed mammal. The rhinoceros is another odd-toed hoofed mammal. Its hooves have three toes. The giraffe is an

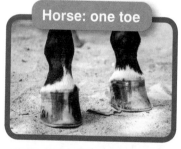
Horse: one toe

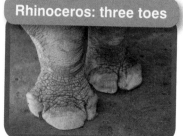
Rhinoceros: three toes

Giraffe: two toes

even-toed mammal. It has two toes on each foot.

The horse's hooves and legs support the weight of the heavy loads some horses carry. A horse's sturdy legs also take the animal over long distances. As horses travel at different speeds, they move their legs in different patterns, called gaits. Basic gaits include trot (slow), canter (fast), and gallop (faster). The horse's ability to speed up quickly helps it escape from possible **predators** or other dangers.

Horses are clever animals. Scientists compare horses' learning abilities to those of apes, dolphins, and elephants. Horses are good communicators, too. They may neigh when they want attention. When frightened, horses often snort. But the main way horses communicate is through body language. Flattened ears or flared nostrils provide clues to a horse's mood. Flattened ears are a sign of anger. Flared nostrils may mean a horse is nervous. A horse with its head lowered is probably relaxed.

COATS AND COLORS An Arabian horse (right) can be one of several different shades of brown, gray, or black. An Appaloosa (left) has a spotted coat.

BREEDS:
A CLOSER LOOK

There are about 400 breeds of horses in the world today. A breed is a group of horses that share certain traits, or characteristics. These traits were passed down from generation to generation. Breeds can be divided into three basic types: heavy horses, light horses, and ponies.

Heavy horses are also known as draft horses or workhorses. These horses are known for their massive size and strength.

Yet they are patient and easy to handle. These gentle giants are good at many types of jobs, such as pulling carriages and plowing fields. Examples of heavy horses include the Percheron (PUR-chuh-rahn), the shire, and the Belgian.

Clydesdales are probably the most famous of the heavy horses. These huge horses can pull weights of nearly 6,000 pounds. They are known for their high-stepping gait and the fancy **feathering** on their lower legs. *Feather* is the term for silky hair on a horse's lower legs.

Shire

Belgian

Clydesdales
are considered
to be **cold-blooded**
horses. The term refers
to their calm and gentle
character.

Clydesdale

Feathering

Light horses are smaller
than their heavy cousins. Riding horses
fall in this category. Popular light breeds
include the Arabian, the American quarter
horse, the Appaloosa, the American paint
horse, and the Thoroughbred.

WHAT'S THE TEMP?

Different breeds are referred to
as **hot-blooded** or cold-blooded.
These terms describe a breed's
temperament (or personality),
not its temperature. After all, all horses—like all
mammals—are **warm-blooded**.

One of the easiest breeds to recognize is the Arabian (see page 12). The Arabian is a light horse with a long, arched neck and a short back. It usually has one fewer **vertebra** (VUR-tuh-bruh), or back bone, than most other breeds! Arabians were first bred to survive in the desert. So these horses are known for their **stamina** (STA-mih-nuh). They are able to bear difficult conditions. Arabians generally take the top prizes in **endurance riding** competitions (races covering very long distances).

The American quarter horse is a short-distance sprinter. It gets its name from its advantage in races on quarter-mile racetracks. If you were asked to close your eyes

American quarter horse

and picture a horse, there's a good chance you'd picture a quarter horse. More than one-third of all the horses in the United States are quarter horses.

Appaloosas are known for their dazzling coats, which come in many colors and patterns. Like snowflakes, no two Appaloosas have the same pattern.

The American paint horse has large splotches of white and another color on its body. Paint horses were common in the Old West, where they were ridden by both cowboys and American Indians. Their patchy coloring could serve as **camouflage** (KA-muh-flahzh).

MARKINGS Many horses have white markings. There are different names for these markings, depending on their shapes and locations. Here are some common markings.

FACIAL MARKINGS

Blaze: a wide white marking down the middle of the face

Stripe: a long, narrow white marking down the middle of the face

Star: a white spot on the center of the forehead

Snip: a white marking between the nostrils

Bald (or whiteface): a face that is mostly white

LEG MARKINGS

Sock: wide white markings from the hoof to below the knee/hock

Stocking: white markings from the hoof to above the knee/hock

Blaze

Stripe

Star

Snip

Bald

Sock

Stocking

The Thoroughbred is the finest racehorse. Running distances of 0.5 to 10 miles, no other breed can beat it. This hot-blooded horse has a strong will and high energy.

Ponies are sometimes confused with **foals**, which are young horses. But being a pony is a matter of size, not age. Ponies are horses that are less than 58 inches tall when fully grown. The Highland pony is one of the largest pony breeds. The Shetland is one of the smallest.

The Highland pony originated in an area of northwestern Scotland known as the Highlands.

LISTEN UP! A horse can turn its ears in the direction a sound is coming from.

SENSES

Horses seem to know when a storm is coming. They may pace or seek shelter before the sky even darkens. They also react to approaching cars long before they come into view. A horse's alert posture and pointed ears may tell its owner that company is on the way. Because horses seem to predict such events before they occur, some people believe they have special senses. They actually have the same five senses we do—vision, hearing, smell, taste, and touch. But some of their senses are much sharper than ours.

VISION The horse's wide, expressive eyes are among the largest in the animal kingdom. Its eyes are bigger than an elephant's! A horse's eyes are located on the sides of its head, which makes its **peripheral** (puh-RIH-fuh-ruhl) **vision** (what it sees off to the sides) very good. When a horse's head is lowered, as it is when it is grazing, it has almost perfect peripheral vision. This helps it keep a watchful eye on its surroundings while it eats.

When its head is upright, a horse has several blind spots. These are areas that it cannot see at all. Horses get startled when

BLIND SPOTS

Can you see your hand when you hold it in front of your face? A horse has a blind spot there and can't see things too close to its face. The gray areas in the image at the right show the places a horse can't see.

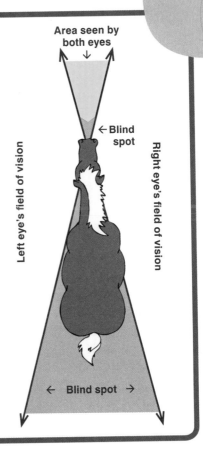

Area seen by both eyes

← Blind spot

Left eye's field of vision

Right eye's field of vision

← Blind spot →

they sense activity in their blind spots. If a horse is approached from behind, it may kick back in fear. That's because the area directly behind a horse is one of its blind spots.

23

HEARING In a hearing contest with humans, horses would win. They can hear higher-pitched  noises than we can. They also hear sounds from greater distances. Their ears rotate to pick up noises coming from different directions. Due to their great sense of hearing, many horses are easily frightened by loud or sudden noises.

SMELL A highly developed sense of smell helps horses in their everyday lives. They recognize people, places, and other animals by smell. Like search-and-

rescue dogs, horses can be trained to follow scents to their sources. They have been used to help find missing persons, too.

TASTE Horses' sense of taste has not been studied very much. We know they tend to like salty and sweet foods and avoid things that taste bitter or

sour. As with most animals (including people), a horse's sense of taste and smell are closely connected. Together, these senses protect horses from eating harmful things, such as poisonous plants, or drinking unclean water. As long as there are other choices available, a horse will avoid drinking or eating things that seem unsafe.

TOUCH Horses are very sensitive to touch. A gentle rub on the forehead or a firm pat on the back means something to a horse. A horse knows these are caring touches.

HORSEY FACE TIME

A SMILE GOES A LONG WAY

Recent research shows that horses may be able to understand human facial expressions. In a 2016 study, psychologists at the University of Sussex showed horses photographs of people with either happy faces or angry faces. When viewing pictures of angry people, the horses showed signs of stress. Their hearts raced, and they shifted their heads to view the photos with their left eyes. Many animals react this way when they feel threatened. The horses did not become stressed when viewing photos of smiling faces. They could tell whether the human facial expression was **positive** (happy) or not.

27

· HORSE SENSE ·

FUNNY FACES

Tapir

Certain scents cause what is known as a horse's **flehmen** (FLAY-mun) **response**. The horse raises its head and curls

Horse

back its upper lip to send the scent to the bottom of its nasal (nose) passages. This "super sniff" can last for several seconds.

This behavior looks strange, but it's perfectly normal. It's how a horse

Rhinoceros

Deer

Tiger

Zebra

investigates an odd or interesting smell. The scent of a female horse commonly causes this reaction in males.

Horses aren't the only animals that do this. Your cat may do it when investigating a new smell. And rhinos, goats, tapirs, and llamas do it, too. Whose flehmen face is the funniest?

Oryx

Goat

MUNCH, MUNCH! Horses are **herbivores**. That means they eat only plants. They **graze** on grass and other low-growing plants.

WHAT'S FOR DINNER?

A horse's main meal consists of fresh grasses and plants. Grass is low in **calories**, a unit of measurement that indicates how much energy is found in food. A food that is high in calories provides more energy. A food that is low in calories provides less energy. So horses need to eat a lot of grass to get the energy their bodies need. For a hungry horse, a field or pasture is like an all-you-can-eat buffet. A horse will spend most of its day grazing. It moves from spot to spot as it eats, searching for the best growth of grass or plants.

Grasses are great horse food, but hay is also good for horses. Hay is grass (or other plant material) that has been cut and dried for use as animal food. It's the main menu item for horses that are kept in stables.

For horses that go outdoors in pastures, snow or other conditions may sometimes prevent grazing. That's when they are fed hay instead. There are many types of hay. Alfalfa, bluegrass, orchard grass, and Bermuda hay are a few popular examples.

WHICH IS WHICH?

Some animals, such as horses, graze. This means they eat grasses and plants on the ground. Other animals, such as deer, **browse**. They eat higher-growing plant matter including shrubs, fruits, and leaves on trees.

33

Many horses, such as working horses, are fed grain in addition to grass or hay. Working horses need to consume extra calories in order to maintain their high energy levels. Some other horses may be given grain just as a treat. Grains include corn, oats, and barley.

Salt is also an important part of a horse's diet, but it's not found in grass or hay. It's usually provided in the form of cubes called **salt licks** that owners give to horses. (Wild horses get salt from natural sources such as plants and soil.)

Fresh fruit and vegetables add vitamins and variety to horse diets. They are especially fond of carrots. Horses also need plenty of clean water to drink.

MEALTIME MANNERS AND TASTY TREATS

A pail hanging on a post is easy to reach.

Horses are often good at sharing food.

A large trough (trawf) has fresh water for all.

Horses like salt and are drawn to salt licks.

Carrots are healthy treats.

How much a horse eats each day depends on its size and activity level. Most horses eat between 1.5 and 2 percent of their body weight in feed each day. That adds up to 15 to 20 pounds for a 1,000-pound horse. A horse as big as a 2,000-pound Clydesdale might eat up to 30 or 40 pounds of food in a single day.

Luckily, a horse's long

teeth were made for grinding grass. Those teeth help the horse chew grass and other foods extremely well before swallowing.

LONG IN THE TOOTH A horse's teeth seem to grow continuously. But they are actually fully formed in its early years. Most of the length is below the gum line. The teeth erupt, or push through the gums,  throughout a horse's lifetime. Wild horses eat rough plants that wear their teeth down. Horses that are fed by people eat softer materials such as hay every day. These horses' teeth need to be filed down. A horse dentist uses a tool called a rasp or float to  make a horse's teeth smooth and even.

The horse has a simple **digestive** (dye-JES-tiv) system compared to that other famous grazer, the cow. Though they both eat mainly grass, their bodies digest, or break down, food differently. Cows have complex, four-part stomachs where most of their food is broken down. After chewing and swallowing grass, they **regurgitate** (ree-GUR-juh-tate) it, or bring it back up to their mouths, to be chewed again.

A horse has just one stomach. But not all food is digested in its stomach. It digests most food in its lower digestive tract, mainly in a part called the **cecum** (SEE-kum). The cecum is a sac located between the large and small intestines.

A horse's cecum is especially large. It contains special **bacteria** (bak-TEER-ee-uh) that help break up all the rough fibers in the plants horses eat.

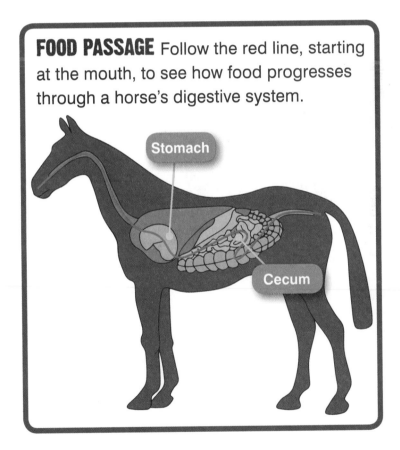

FOOD PASSAGE Follow the red line, starting at the mouth, to see how food progresses through a horse's digestive system.

Stomach

Cecum

FACT FILE: HOW DO YOU DOO?

Anyone who has been around horses knows they poop a lot. A horse produces six to eight piles of poop, called **manure** (muh-NOOR), in a single day. That's a lot of poop to scoop!

The term for cleaning a **stall** is *mucking out*. That's because *muck* is another word for manure. Mucking out is usually done with a pitchfork, shovel, and wheelbarrow. Manure and dirty bedding (usually straw or wood shavings) should be removed from a horse's stall every day.

Horse manure can be great **fertilizer** (a substance that makes soil richer so plants grow better). Dried bricks made of manure can be burned for fuel.

One animal's poop may be another's soup. Tiger swallowtail butterflies are attracted to salty things such as this pile of manure.

BONDED A mare stays close to her newborn foal. She is **protective** and may try to kick or bite a person or another horse that comes too close.

CHAPTER 5

FAMILY LIFE

Meet the members of the horse family. A **mare** is an adult female horse. An adult male is known as a **stallion**. Stallions are usually slightly larger than mares. A baby horse (from birth through one year of age) is called a foal. A young female is a **filly**; a young male is a **colt**. Horses are usually considered mature at five years of age.

A mare can have one baby each year. She is pregnant for eleven months before a foal is born. The baby horse can walk within hours of being born. Its first steps are wobbly, but before long it can follow its mother around. It sticks very close to her for the next month. During this time, a foal depends on its mother for protection and food. Its nourishment comes from its mother's milk.

Horses are highly social animals. They prefer being in the company of other horses, both for friendship and for safety. Free-roaming horses live in **herds**. A herd is made up of smaller groups known as bands. A band usually consists of a few mares, their foals, and one stallion. Members of a band spend most of their time together. They may wander off from the herd, but

QUICK LEARNER A mother keeps an eye on her foal as it starts to crawl. The foal pulls itself forward with its front legs. A bit wobbly, it pushes up until it is standing. All this happens in its first 20 to 30 minutes.

usually they don't stray too far. Band members don't stay in the same group forever. As with human friendships, some last longer than others.

A group of horses has clear leaders and followers. Each individual has a rank or position in the **hierarchy** (HYE-ur-ahr-kee), the organization of the group. The highest-ranking horse makes decisions about group movements and who eats first. The leader isn't necessarily the biggest or oldest horse. A horse becomes a leader by its behavior. A submissive horse tends to back down when challenged. A **dominant** horse usually wins fights. For a long time, many people believed that stallions were the natural leaders of wild herds. But experts now believe that females are often the ones in charge.

Family ties play a big part in where others rank within the group. If a particular mare is the leader, her foal will probably be a high-ranking member of the group. The **offspring** of a low-ranking mare will most likely never become the boss. The saying "You scratch my back, and I'll scratch yours" means doing something nice for someone, hoping that person will return the favor. In the world of horses, actually scratching each other's backs is a sign of friendship. Horses groom each other by nibbling at the other's upper neck, back, and withers. This is an important aspect of a horse's social life. Grooming strengthens relationships between horses.

SPECIAL DELIVERY In the wild, doctors aren't around to help animals have their babies. But a pregnant horse's owner will make sure a veterinarian is on call—just in case an emergency arises. A mare that is ready to have a foal usually wants to be alone. She is moved into a large **foaling stall** or separate penned-in area when her due date approaches. Clean straw on the ground provides comfortable bedding. The birthing process takes less than an hour. A foal usually shares its mother's stall while it is nursing (drinking its mother's milk). This period lasts about four to six months.

READY...SET...GO!
A birthing alarm, such as this one on a belt around the midsection, alerts the owner when a horse is ready to give birth.

AGES AND STAGES

Foal

Horses live an average of 25 to 30 years. By the age of five, they're considered adults. They grow more quickly than humans do. But like people, their early years have different stages.

From birth to one year, a young horse is called a foal. It stays close to its mother, nursing for the first four to six months.

A **yearling** is between one and two years old. It is learning basic skills, such as getting

Yearling

along with others and standing still for grooming.

A colt is a male horse from two to four years old.

A filly is a female horse from two to four years old.

Colt and filly

If a colt or filly is going to be ridden, it will be trained during these years. By the time colts and fillies reach adulthood at age five, most are their full size and weight.

HOME SWEET HOME
A barn or **stable** is a place for a horse to sleep, eat, and be with other animals and people.

BARN AND STABLE

Housing is as important for horses as it is for humans. Unless they are **feral** (FEH-rul), or wild, most horses spend at least part of their time in stables. A stable is the most common form of shelter for a horse. A proper stable is clean and dry and provides protection from poor weather. It has good ventilation, allowing fresh air to flow through the building.

Some horses spend most of their time in fields or pastures. They go indoors only at nighttime or when the weather is very bad. (Most horses don't mind being in a little bit of rain or snow. But they prefer to be sheltered from thunderstorms.) Other horses live in stables full-time, with short periods of **turnout** each day. Turnout is the time a horse spends outside in a pasture, field, or **corral** (kuh-RAL). Spending time

RECESS A **paddock**, also called a corral or pen, provides safe outdoor space for horses. They can graze, exercise, and enjoy the fresh air.

outdoors is important for a horse's health and well-being.

A stable is divided into stalls. A horse's stall is like its bedroom. Most stables have more stalls than the number of horses there. This helps in different ways. When a horse's stall needs to be cleaned, the horse can be switched to an empty one. Also, if two horses aren't

getting along, they might need an empty stall between them. Of course, bigger horses need bigger stalls. A Clydesdale's stall should be at least twice the size of a stall meant for a pony. When a mare has a foal, they are usually kept together in an extra-roomy foaling stall for at least the first few months.

Water and feed buckets are usually hung on the wall rather than placed on the

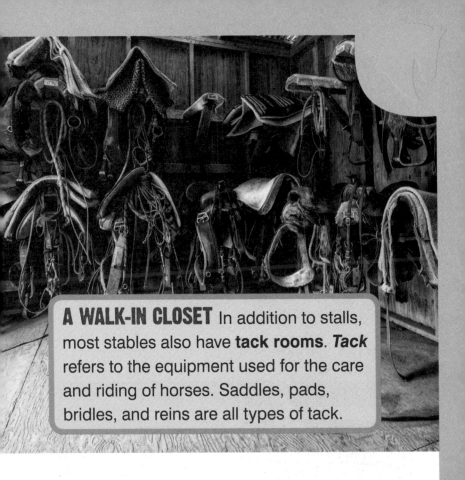

A WALK-IN CLOSET In addition to stalls, most stables also have **tack rooms**. *Tack* refers to the equipment used for the care and riding of horses. Saddles, pads, bridles, and reins are all types of tack.

ground where the horse could kick them over. Hay bags or hay nets may be hung on the wall, too. But some horses do eat hay from buckets or tubs on the ground.

While stalls vary in size and features, they should always include windows or other openings that allow the horses to look out. Horses want to know what's going on in their surroundings. As social animals, they also like to see and communicate with others. Many stall doors are designed so that the top half can swing open even when the bottom is closed. This allows a horse to view and **nuzzle** (rub noses with) its neighbor.

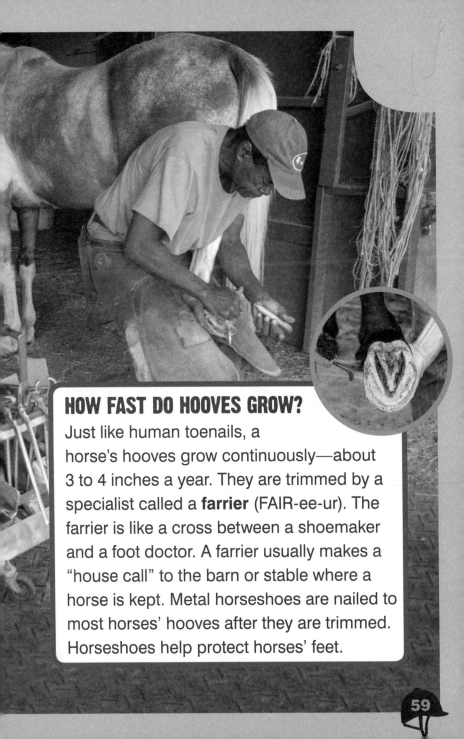

HOW FAST DO HOOVES GROW?

Just like human toenails, a horse's hooves grow continuously—about 3 to 4 inches a year. They are trimmed by a specialist called a **farrier** (FAIR-ee-ur). The farrier is like a cross between a shoemaker and a foot doctor. A farrier usually makes a "house call" to the barn or stable where a horse is kept. Metal horseshoes are nailed to most horses' hooves after they are trimmed. Horseshoes help protect horses' feet.

FACT FILE: BUDDY SYSTEM?

If a horse is nervous by nature, a buddy can help keep it calm. Horses are social animals and they may make friends with other animals on a farm, too. The best buddy isn't always another horse!

PONIES Ponies are popular horse pals. When kept for companionship, they are known as stable ponies or barn ponies.

DONKEYS Donkeys are not horses, but they are related. Donkeys tend to be calm and curious.

GOATS Goats are also herd animals, and they get along well with horses.

DOGS AND CATS Dogs and cats are popular on farms. Some live in stables to keep the horses company.

MULES A mule is an offspring of a horse and a donkey. These two look like best pals.

IT TAKES TWO Horseback riding is a team effort. Whether competing, trail riding, or bringing in a herd, the rider and the horse work together.

CHAPTER 7

HORSEBACK RIDING

For most of human history, the fastest way to travel was on horseback. Today, the car has replaced the horse as our top choice for ground transportation. Yet horseback riding remains a popular pastime. There are two main types of riding: **Western** and **English**. Both styles are practiced around the world. Each has its own equipment, clothing, customs, and events. In general, Western riding is casual, while English riding is more formal.

Picture a cowboy riding on a ranch. He holds both reins in one hand. In the other hand he holds a rope to lasso, or round up, cattle. His horse's saddle is wide and heavy, with a horn (or knob)

HEAD 'EM UP, MOVE 'EM OUT
Horses and riders work together to round up herds of buffalo.

in front. The horn may be used to tie down a rope or as a handle for the rider. This is an example of Western (casual) riding. Most parade horses are ridden Western style, too.

Now picture a rider gracefully guiding her horse around obstacles (such as rocks, logs, and holes) along a riding path in the countryside. The rider holds one rein in each hand. Her horse's saddle is small and has no horn. The horse can move about and jump without being weighed down by a bulky saddle. This is an example of English (formal) riding.

While some people ride horses in either style purely

for pleasure, others take part in competitions. A **horse show** is an event in which riders show off their horses' skills. Judges decide on a winner. There are many types of horse shows, each focusing on a different breed of horse or activity.

A **rodeo** (ROH-dee-oh) is a demonstration of Western riding skills. Rodeos occur worldwide but are most commonly seen in the western United States. Competitive rodeo events include **cattle roping** and **barrel racing**.

Cattle roping tests a rider's ability to lasso a cow. The rider does this by tossing a rope around the cow's horns or legs. The rider who ropes the fastest wins. In barrel racing, riders race their horses around barrels to see who can complete the run in the fastest time.

The **steeplechase** competition has a course that is spread out over a few miles. In this race, obstacles may include natural objects, such as trees and streams, as well as jumps created for the event.

Steeplechase

Dressage

Dressage (druh-SAHZH) shows off an elegant style of riding, featuring the horse doing fancy footwork and high steps. Dressage is often described as ballet on horseback. Horses that perform in dressage events are highly trained. In fact, the word *dressage* means "training" in French.

English riding shows are held around the world, including at the Summer Olympics. One of the most popular

IN THE TACK ROOM

Saddles, bridles, and other equipment needed for horseback riding is called tack. Here are examples of tack found at an English-style riding stable.

Saddle

Saddle pad

Stirrup

Blanket

Bridle

Horseshoes

Brush

Protection boots

Show jumping

events is **show jumping**. Most horses can easily leap over small objects. But only the most athletic and agile (AJ-il), or quick, horses compete in show jumping. In this event, riders guide their horses over a series of obstacles. Show jumping obstacles include fences and poles of various heights and widths.

Polo is a sport played with two teams of riders on small horses. From

Polo

horseback, players use mallets to hit a ball into the opposing team's goal.

Endurance riding competitions test a horse's stamina, or staying ability, as well as the rider's skills. These contests cover long distances—up to 100 miles. Some take place during a single day, while longer races may last a few days.

Endurance riding

FACT FILE: RIDING IN STYLE!

You can tell Western and English riders apart by their clothing. English riders dress formally, especially in competition. Some English riding events, such as dressage, require specific uniforms or colors. Western riding has a more relaxed look.

Hacking jacket

Hunt cap or helmet

Cowboy hat

Western-style shirt

Neckerchief

Spurs

Jodhpurs   Riding boots   Cowboy boots   Chaps

English   Western

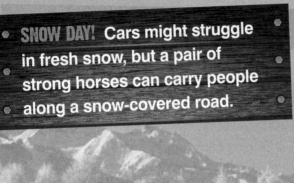

SNOW DAY! Cars might struggle in fresh snow, but a pair of strong horses can carry people along a snow-covered road.

WORKING HORSES

A police horse carries an officer through a city crowd. A pair of Percheron horses pulls a plow across a farmer's field. A shire horse wearing a special harness hauls logs from the woods. These are just a few examples of work performed by horses around the world.

Working horses are also called draft horses. Draft horses are the tallest and strongest breeds. Each can weigh more than a ton. These huge horses can carry loads several times their weight. Once upon a time, they provided most of the labor used in farming and transportation. Today, machines and motor vehicles have replaced animals in many jobs. But working horses are still found on farms, on ranches, and in other settings.

FARMING Not all farmers traded their horses for tractors in the last century. Horses remain in use on many small and

family farms. In fact, their popularity is growing now. Many farmers believe that horse-powered farming costs less than farming done with machines and is better for the environment. But most large-scale **agricultural** (a-grih-KUL-chuh-rul) businesses still rely on machines, which can get jobs done faster.

LOGGING Loggers chop down trees and cut them into logs, or lumber. Draft horses help loggers gather

up and move lumber. These horses are used because they are able to **maneuver** (muh-NOO-vur), move skillfully, around trees better than a tractor can.

RANCHING A horse that works with livestock (such as cattle and oxen) is called a **stock horse**. Ranchers use stock horses to herd animals, or guide them from place to place. After grazing in one area for a while, a herd of cattle will need to be moved to greener pastures. When winter approaches, herds are moved from cold regions to warmer ones.

Cows may be spread out over large areas of unpaved land. It would be very difficult for a rancher on foot or in a car to round up, or gather, these animals. Horses help the rancher move cattle from one pasture to another. A horse with a skill for herding cattle is said to have "cow sense."

In the mid-1800s,

millions of cattle were herded from ranches out West to markets and railways in the East. These cattle drives have been featured in many Western movies. They are part of the image of the American cowboy. Cattle drives still occur today. But these events are more for entertainment than anything else.

LAW ENFORCEMENT Some cities and towns still have **mounted police**.

Officers on horseback can move down narrow alleys and other places a squad car can't reach.

Sitting so high up helps them spot possible trouble farther away.

TRANSPORTATION Horses can still be seen pulling carriages in many places around the world. This form of transportation is especially popular with tourists in large cities. A horse and carriage easily take people from one place to another. Clydesdales are often used as

carriage horses. They are super-strong, and the feathering on their legs gives them an elegant appearance.

NATIONAL PARKS Horses are valued members of the crew at many national parks. Rangers on horseback patrol rough or steep terrain (ground). Horses carry equipment and supplies for park rangers. They may also help rescue people in danger.

Many national parks allow visitors to explore the wilderness on horseback. These horse-friendly parks often have their own stables and offer guided trail rides.

FACT FILE: LATIN AMERICAN COWBOYS

Cowboys are part of the cultures of Mexico and Central and South America, where they go by different names. These are just a few examples.

VAQUEROS (Mexico): Mexico's livestock herders are known for their roping skills. They helped shape the American cowboy tradition.

GAUCHOS (Argentina and other countries): There are lots of *gauchos* in Argentina, where cattle herding is a big business.

CHAGRAS

(Ecuador): The main job of the *chagras* is to round up bulls in the mountains of Ecuador.

MOROCHUCOS

(Peru): Clothing made from alpaca wool helps these cowboys deal with the cold weather in the Andes Mountains.

LLANEROS

(Venezuela and Colombia): These cattle herders get their name from the grasslands (Los Llanos) where they live.

THE WILD WEST Free-roaming horses are a reflection of the pioneering American spirit. There are 170 wild horse and burro herds on public lands in ten western states. They are currently protected by a U.S. government agency called the Bureau of Land Management.

WILD ONES

When people speak of wild horses, they often mean mustangs. Thousands of mustangs roam free in the western United States. But these horses are not truly wild. The proper word to describe them is *feral*. They are descendants of tame horses that escaped from Spanish explorers more than 400 years ago.

Mustangs come in all colors— including black, brown, chestnut, gray, and palomino (pa-luh-MEE-noh), or gold with a white mane and tail. Most have small bodies (13 to 14.2 hands high). They are tough animals, built to survive in desert environments.

Feral horses also live on a few islands off the coast of the eastern United States. The most famous of these are the Assateague (A-suh-teeg) ponies. These small horses live on Assateague, an island that borders both Maryland and Virginia. According to legend, the first horses to arrive on the island were survivors of a Spanish shipwreck. But there is no evidence to back up that interesting story. The horses' true beginnings on the island are unknown.

Though they live on Assateague, these animals

HORSEY PADDLE The annual Pony Swim, begun in 1924, attracts thousands of spectators in boats and along the shoreline.

are often called Chincoteague (SHING-kuh-teeg) ponies. That's because once a year, the ponies on Assateague are rounded up to swim over to nearby Chincoteague Island. There, the foals are auctioned off to raise money to support the herd's upkeep. Spectators wait for up to five hours to watch the ponies make the five-minute swim!

Free-roaming horses are also found on Georgia's Cumberland Island. The

SMALL IN NUMBER Only about 100 wild horses live on Cumberland Island.

first horses may have been brought to Cumberland Island by Spanish missionaries in the 1500s. Today's Cumberland Island horses are a mix of many breeds, including Tennessee walkers, American quarter horses, Arabians, and Paso Finos.

Sable Island, off the coast of Nova Scotia, Canada, is home to another breed of feral horse. Sable Island horses are short

and shaggy. Thick coats help protect them during the island's harsh winters.

The Camargue (kah-MAHRG) horse is a small, feral breed native to southern

FAST BEAUTIES Nicknamed "horses of the sea," Camargues love to gallop in the water.

France. Foals are born black or brown. But these beautiful horses have white coats when fully grown.

Another feral horse, the brumby, lives in the outback—the rugged interior of the Australian **continent**. The brumby's ancestors were horses that escaped from gold mining camps in the mid-1800s. Since then, their numbers have greatly increased. They are tough, fast-moving horses.

SLEEK STALLION
Brumbies come in all colors and coat patterns.

HOW DOES A HORSE SAY "BACK OFF"?

TAIL SWISHING A swishing tail is useful to swat away flies. Fast, repeated swishing may indicate anger.

REARING Rising to its full height, a horse can signal its role as the dominant or lead animal in a herd. This may be enough to scare off challengers or predators.

KICKING A horse kicks in self-defense. It's a way to shoo away an intruder or predator.

SPARRING When two horses spar, or fight, they look fierce. The fight ends when one horse backs down.

BUCKING This instinctive behavior is a way for a horse to get something— such as a pouncing cougar or an unwanted rider—off its back. The horse first lowers its head and raises its back, then lifts up its **hindquarters**. A buck often ends in a leg kick.

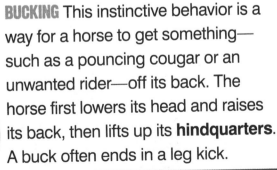

The only truly wild horse living today is the Przewalski's (shuh-VAHL-skeez) horse of Mongolia. This wild horse with the hard-to-pronounce name has an amazing story. Przewalski's horses were never tamed by humans. In the 1960s, they were declared extinct in the wild—there were none left in nature. But several lived in places such as zoos and animal parks. Offspring of these animals have now been released to the wild. Today, more than 300 Przewalski's horses are living free in their Mongolian homeland. The only reason these animals exist today is that people cared about their survival and made a plan to save them.

FACT FILE: MEET THE FAMILY

Like horses, these animals are members of the genus *Equus*. That means they are the horse's closest relatives.

DONKEY A donkey is a tamed version of the African wild ass.

ZEBRA Scientists recognize three types of zebras: mountain, plains, and Grevy's.

WILD ASS Wild asses are found in Africa and Asia. Types include the

onager (also known as the Asiatic wild ass) and the kiang (sometimes called the Tibetan wild ass).

A PERFECT FIT The first horse a young person rides might be a pony. It's just the right size— not too big and not too small.

PONIES AND MINIS

"Enjoy the little things" is a common saying. And fans of ponies and miniature horses (also called "minis") certainly do just that. These little animals are enormously popular.

Ponies and miniature horses look similar. But there are several differences between them. The most obvious is their size. A pony is a small horse, less than 58 inches tall. A mini is an *even smaller* horse, no more than 38 inches tall. A mini might be only about the size of a large dog, such as a Great Dane.

These animals have different body types, too. Ponies tend to have short legs and wide bodies. Their coats, manes, and tails are thicker than horses'. A mini looks like a horse that has been zapped by a shrinking wand. It has the same body type as a horse, only smaller. Most ponies can be ridden by adults as well as children. These small animals have stronger backs than miniature horses do. Minis cannot carry a lot of weight on their backs. They should be ridden only by small children.

You will frequently see ponies at fairs, festivals, and carnivals. Minis make great show animals. Both minis and ponies are common on family farms.

Many people insist that miniature horses are ponies. That's because a pony is defined as *any* horse under 58 inches tall. Not everyone agrees. However, one thing is certain: the two are closely related. One of the miniature horse's ancestors is actually the Shetland pony.

PONY BREEDS There are dozens of pony breeds. The American Shetland is the most popular pony in the United States. The Shetland is a small but powerful pony. It stands up to 42 inches tall.

The Hackney makes a great show pony. It

Hackney

Fjord

is known for its high-stepping gait.

The Fjord (fee-ORD) is one of the oldest breeds. A Fjord is solid tan or brown, with a black stripe down the center of the mane and tail.

The Pony of the Americas has a spotted coat. Its narrow back makes it easy for a child to ride.

Pony of the Americas

MINI BREEDS The first miniature horse breed was the Falabella. Falabellas are rare outside of South America. They have long tails and manes and

Falabella

are intelligent animals.

The American miniature horse comes in a wide variety of colors. Solid colors include black, gray, buckskin (golden), and sorrel (reddish). Some minis have Appaloosa (spotted) or pinto (splotchy) markings. Miniature horses are strong for their size. Some are also considered members of other breeds. For example, miniature Arabians are thought to be members of both the miniature horse family and the Arabian horse family.

American miniature horse

CAN HORSES BE HELPERS? The miniature horse is recognized as a service animal by a special law known as the Americans with Disabilities Act. Thanks to their small size and sweet nature, minis can be trained to help people with special needs.

HEROIC HORSES

Therapy horses are heroes of the animal world. An American miniature horse named Magic visits places where people need cheering up, such as hospitals and nursing homes. Spending time with Magic takes patients' minds off their illnesses or other problems. On one visit, Magic met an elderly woman who hadn't said a word in three years. But once she saw Magic, the old woman began to speak again. "Isn't she beautiful?" she asked.

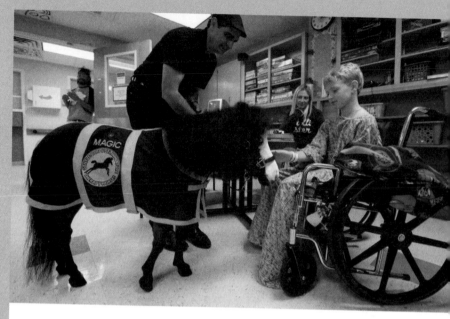

Magic has changed the lives of many people. TIME magazine called Magic one of the ten most courageous animals in history. That's a big honor for a little horse!

Horses form meaningful connections with people. That's why they make excellent therapy animals. Horse therapy is very helpful for kids with autism (AW-tiz-um). Children with autism may have difficulty with communication and motor skills. Being with and riding horses helps them improve these skills. It also lowers stress levels and builds confidence.

Horses have a long history of traveling with soldiers to war. Reckless was the name of a chestnut mare that served with the U.S. Marines during the Korean War, in the 1950s. She delivered supplies to troops in battle. She also took wounded soldiers away from harm. She was

Reckless with her foal Fearless

wounded twice, too. Reckless earned numerous medals and was given the important title of staff sergeant. She is one of few horses in history to be buried with full military honors.

A mixed-breed horse named Comanche (kuh-MAN-shee) was the only member of General George Armstrong Custer's troops to survive the famous Battle of the Little Bighorn, in Montana in 1876. Comanche was badly wounded, but he was nursed back to health. The horse was treated

Comanche and General George Armstrong Custer

like royalty for the rest of his days.

Many heroic horses never become famous names. In 2009, huge bushfires broke out in Victoria, Australia. In that area, a retired Thoroughbred racehorse named Fabish shared a paddock on a farm with seven yearlings. The young horses were frightened by the approaching flames. The farm manager opened the gates so the horses could flee.

Fire destroyed the farm, and the horses were feared dead. But the next morning, Fabish returned—with the others following behind him, single file. The old horse had led the yearlings to safety and then brought them home. His story was told in a book for young readers called *Fabish: The Horse That Braved a Bushfire.*

IN THE SPOTLIGHT

Meet a few horses who have galloped their way to fame:

A palomino named Trigger appeared in many movies and on television shows during the 1940s and 1950s. He starred alongside his owner, cowboy superstar Roy Rogers. Trigger was a very intelligent horse. He learned to perform many tricks and stunts for the movies.

Mister Ed was a television series about a talking horse. It was one of the most popular comedy shows of the 1960s. A horse

named Bamboo Harvester played the role of Ed. Bamboo Harvester was an American saddlebred-Arabian mix.

Misty of Chincoteague was a real pony that inspired a bestselling book. Author Marguerite Henry met Misty on a visit to Chincoteague Island. She purchased Misty from her owners, the Beebe family. Misty was 12 hands (48 inches) tall. White markings on her side looked like a map of the United States. Following the success of *Misty of Chincoteague*, Marguerite Henry wrote other books based on the island's ponies.

GLOSSARY

agricultural Having to do with farming.

bacteria Tiny, single-celled organisms. Some bacteria can cause disease.

barrel racing A rodeo event in which riders race their horses around barrels, making many sharp turns.

browse To feed on plants above the ground, such as shrubs or leaves on trees.

calorie A measurement of the energy found in food.

camouflage A natural coloring that helps animals hide by making them blend in with their surroundings.

cattle roping A rodeo event in which a rider chases and lassos a young cow.

cecum A sac inside a horse or other plant-eating animal, located between the large and small intestines, that stores helpful bacteria.

cold-blooded Having a calm and gentle character.

colt A young male horse.

continent One of seven large landmasses on Earth: Asia, Africa, Europe, North America, South America, Australia, and Antarctica.

corral A fenced-in area for catching and holding animals.

digest To break down food into simpler forms that can be taken in and used by the body. A horse has a simple digestive system with one stomach.

dominant Having power or influence over others.

dressage An elegant style of horse riding in which a trained horse and rider perform a series of fancy movements.

endurance riding Riding horseback for long hours over long distances.

English riding A form of horse riding with European military roots. An English rider uses a small, light saddle and often wears a helmet, a tie, a jacket, breeches, and riding boots.

farrier A person who puts shoes on horses.

feathering The long hair on the lower legs of some breeds of horses.

feral Wild. Feral horses live freely, but their ancestors were once tamed.

fertilizer A substance added to soil to help crops grow.

filly A young female horse.

flehmen response A behavior in which a mammal breathes in with the mouth open and upper lip curled to take in scents.

foal A young horse of either sex.

foaling stall A private penned-in area where a female horse can give birth.

graze To feed on grass and plants from the ground.

herbivore An animal that eats only plants.

herd A group of animals that lives or is kept together.

hierarchy A system in which people, animals, or things are organized based on their various levels of importance.

hindquarters The back pair of legs of a four-legged animal.

horse show An exhibition of horses that usually includes riding and jumping contests and races.

hot-blooded Having an angry or excitable character.

maneuver To move carefully or skillfully.

manure Animal poop that is used as fertilizer or fuel.

mare An adult female horse.

mounted police Police who patrol on horseback.

muck out To clean a horse's stall. Mucking out is usually done with a pitchfork, shovel, and wheelbarrow.

nuzzle To touch or rub with the nose or mouth.

offspring The young of an animal or person.

paddock A fenced-in area where animals can graze or exercise.

peripheral vision What the eyes can see to the sides when looking straight ahead.

polo A team sport played on horseback. Players try to hit a small ball using long wooden mallets.

positive Happy or approving.

predator An animal that hunts and eats other animals.

protective Feeling driven to keep someone or something safe from harm. Mares are protective of their foals.

regurgitate To bring chewed and swallowed food back up to the mouth.

rodeo A demonstration of Western riding skills. Competitors try to ride wild horses and lasso cows.

rotate To move in a circle around a central point.

salt lick A block of salt given to an animal that provides important nutrients when the animal licks it.

show jumping The competitive sport of riding a horse through an obstacle course in an arena.

species A category of living things with similar traits that can mate and have offspring together.

stable A building in which farm animals are fed and housed.

stall A compartment for one animal in a stable.

stallion An adult male horse.

stamina The energy and strength to keep doing something without weakening.

steeplechase An event in which horses race across countryside, jumping over ditches and hedges.

stock horse A horse used to help herd cattle on a ranch.

tack Equipment needed for riding horses, such as saddles, pads, bridles, and reins.

tack room A room in or attached to a stable for the storage and maintenance of riding tack.

temperament Personality. A horse's temperament is described as either hot-blooded or cold-blooded.

turnout The time a horse spends outdoors, not in a stable.

vertebra One of the small bones that make up the spine.

vertebrate An animal with a backbone. Mammals, fish, amphibians, reptiles, and birds are all vertebrates.

warm-blooded Able to maintain a constant body temperature regardless of the temperature of the environment. Horses, like all mammals, are warm-blooded.

Western riding A form of horse riding that developed according to the needs of cowboys. A Western rider uses a saddle with a deep seat and often wears a traditional western hat, a comfortable shirt, jeans, and western-style boots.

withers The ridge between a horse's shoulders.

yearling A horse that is between one and two years old.

RESOURCES

Learn more about horses by visiting museums and zoos.
Many national parks have riding trails, and some offer
lessons or trail rides. Check out informative websites.
And read more books like this one.

WHERE TO SEE WILD HORSES

Here are a few places to see wild horses:
* Take a ferry from St. Marys, Georgia, to Cumberland Island,
  where you can see wild horses, often on the beach.
* Visit the Pryor Mountain Wild Mustang Center in Wyoming to
  learn about the most recent location of wild horse herds.
* Visit the Theodore Roosevelt National Park in North Dakota,
  where wild horses travel in bands (small groups).
* Watch beautiful wild horses roam through tropical valleys and
  waterfalls in Waipi'o Valley, Hawaii.
* Many zoos have wild horses, including the San Diego, Minnesota,
  and Bronx Zoos.

MUSEUMS AND WEBSITES

Appaloosa Museum &
Heritage Center
Moscow, ID
appaloosamuseum.com

American Saddlebred
Museum
Lexington, KY
asbmuseum.org

International Museum of
the Horse
   Lexington, KY
    imh.org

Pony Express National Museum
St. Joseph, MO
ponyexpress.org

National Cowboy & Western
Heritage Museum
Oklahoma City, OK
nationalcowboymuseum.org

National Cowgirl Museum and
Hall of Fame
Fort Worth, TX
cowgirl.net

Wild Horse and Burro Program
*blm.gov/programs/wild-horse-
and-burro*

BOOKS

Animals: A Visual Encyclopedia, by Animal Planet
(Animal Planet/Time Inc. Books)

Animal Bites: Farm Animals, by Animal Planet
(Animal Planet/Time Inc. Books)

Animal Planet Adventures: Farm Friends Escape,
by Gail Herman (Animal Planet/Time Inc. Books)

CREDITS AND ACKNOWLEDGMENTS

Writer Brenda Scott Royce
Produced by Scout Books & Media Inc
President and Project Director Susan Knopf
Project Manager Brittany Gialanella
Copyeditor Stephanie Engel
Proofreader Melanie Petsch
Designer Annemarie Redmond
Advisors Michael Rentz, PhD, *Lecturer in Mammalogy, Iowa State University*; Leslie Clapper-Rentz, DVM, *Small Animal and Exotics Veterinarian*

Thanks to the Time Inc. Books team: Margot Schupf, Anja Schmidt, Beth Sutinis, Deirdre Langeland, Hillary Leary, Georgia Morrissey, Megan Pearlman, and Nina Reed.

Special thanks to everyone at Discovery Global Enterprises.

PHOTO CREDITS